STONE COLD MURDER

STONE COLD MURDER
by James Cawood

JOSEF WEINBERGER PLAYS

LONDON

STONE COLD MURDER
First published in 2014
by Josef Weinberger Ltd
12-14 Mortimer Street, London W1T 3JJ
www.josef-weinberger.com / plays@jwmail.co.uk

ISBN: 978 0 85676 334 2

Printed by Berforts Information Press Ltd, Stevenage, UK

For Mum and Dad

STONE COLD MURDER was first presented at Vienna's English Theatre on 28th March 2011. The cast was as follows:

OLIVIA	Fliss Walton
ROBERT	William Findlay
RAMSAY	Matthew Rutherford
SAM	David Partridge

Directed by Andy de la Tour

Set and costumes designed by Sue Mayes

CHARACTERS

OLIVIA

ROBERT

RAMSAY

SAM

ACT ONE

The entrance hall / living room of The Langstrath Country House Hotel in the English Lake District. A desolate spot, surrounded by mountains at the head of a valley. A dusty, oak dominated room. Stone-flagged floor, with rug. Wall-mounted lights dimly illuminate corners of the room. A leather sofa and a leather puff, worn in and soft. SR: A small corridor that leads to the front door and stairs up to the bedrooms. By the hallway entrance is an upright chair and on the wall DS of it hangs a full length mirror. Between the hallway entrance and the stairs is the reception desk, the sort the proprietor stands behind whilst checking in guests. On top of this sits a phone, a lamp and a guest book. There is also a small cash box hidden behind the desk. On the back wall, centre stage is a pair of French windows with curtains, so that when drawn the windows are hidden. As the lights come up they are not drawn. These windows lead into the hotel's garden, used in summer. Next to these is a pair of heavy boots. SL: By the wall is a wood burning stove with the dying embers of the day's blaze glowing. Next to this: a poker and a small log basket, nearly empty. Next to this is a small and simple drinks cabinet upon which sits a CD player and some CDs.

Present day. January. Deep winter in the Lake District. As the curtain comes up, all we hear is the whistling of a strong wind, gusting and whipping around the old building. The room is dimly lit. About 7.00 p.m. Silence. Suddenly, the wind-whipped silence is shattered by the shrill ring of the telephone. It continues to ring for a few moments before . . .

Enter OLIVIA *from the bedrooms. She is wearing old jeans, woolly jumper and socks; dressed for a night by the fireplace. She is just about to answer the phone when it stops ringing. She shakes her head, yawns and stretches. The phone starts to ring again. She answers the phone.*

OLIVIA   Langstrath Country House Hotel. Olivia
                spea . . . Hello? Hello?

(She takes the receiver from her ear and looks at it, then hangs up. Uneasy. Enter ROBERT *from the bedrooms, also dressed comfortably. He comes in yawning and stretching from his nap. Tousled hair.)*

ROBERT   Hello there . . .

OLIVIA   (*forgetting any concern*) Oh . . . You look adorable.

ROBERT   Well, I try my best.

OLIVIA   I think we nodded off.

ROBERT   Yes, we did.

(She puts her arms around his waist and rests her head on his shoulder.)

OLIVIA   It's Radio Four you know, these plays they put on. Send you straight off to sleep.

ROBERT   Don't tell the author that. At least I woke up in time to find out who the murderer was.

OLIVIA   And who was it?

ROBERT   A chap named Durbridge.

OLIVIA   Durbridge?

ROBERT   Yes. Don't have a clue who he is. We must have drifted off before he appeared.

OLIVIA   Very wise . . . when it comes to murderers.

ROBERT   Quite. Can't feel bad about it, though.

OLIVIA   What?

(OLIVIA *goes over to the wall and puts the lights on.*)

ROBERT   Falling asleep in the evening. We've had a great season, we've been rushed off our feet and now we're on holiday.

OLIVIA   On holiday, yes.

ROBERT   Drink?

OLIVIA   Why not.

ROBERT   We're on holiday.

OLIVIA   Yes.

(ROBERT *goes to a small drinks cabinet next to the fireplace and produces a bottle of gin, some tonic and two glasses. He holds one of them up and inspects it. It is different from the other.*)

ROBERT   We've been married for six months now and I still don't know why you insist on having the same glass every time you have a drink.

OLIVIA   I told you, it was my mother's. I like using it. It makes me feel . . . I don't know.

(*He pours the drinks. Gin and Tonic, twice.*)

ROBERT   Do you miss her?

OLIVIA   Mum? Yes, sometimes. You know, after ten years one gets used to it I suppose, but sometimes I would just like . . .

ROBERT   What?

OLIVIA   A chat.

ROBERT   A chat?

OLIVIA   Yes, you know to talk to her. Ask some
                advice. She always gave the best advice.

ROBERT   (*handing her the drink*) Better than me?

OLIVIA   Oh yes, darling. You're a vagabond, a real
                scoundrel. You give terrible advice.

ROBERT   Ha! A scoundrel . . . I wish.

OLIVIA   (*sidling up to him*) I'm glad you're not. I'm
                glad you're just plain old Robert.

ROBERT   Thank you.

ROBERT   Cheers.

OLIVIA   Cheers.

                (*They drink.*)

ROBERT   Would she have liked me?

OLIVIA   (*sitting on the sofa and stretching her legs
                out almost seductively*) Of course she would.
                She would have positively adored you.

ROBERT   Glad you think so.

OLIVIA   I wouldn't have married you so quickly
                otherwise.

ROBERT   We were rather quick, weren't we?

OLIVIA   Just a bit. Married after a month? People
                must have thought us mad.

ROBERT   Not now though.

OLIVIA   No, they probably think us even loopier for
                coming up to the middle of nowhere and
                buying a crumbling old hotel.

ROBERT   Not likely.

OLIVIA   No?

ROBERT   No. Just look how well we've done. Our first
                season and with a little advertising and a
                lot of word of mouth, we almost doubled the
                profits of the old owners.

OLIVIA   Not hard, though. I'm surprised those two
                didn't sell the tiles from the roof they were
                in so much debt.

ROBERT   With a wind like this, I'm surprised there
                are any tiles to sell.

                (*Silence.*)

ROBERT   Should I get some more wood for the stove?

OLIVIA   Oh, stay here for bit. We never get the
                chance to relax in here when we have
                guests, we may as well make the most of it
                while we can.

ROBERT   Yes, I suppose.

                (*Pause.* OLIVIA *glances at the telephone.*)

OLIVIA   We could take the phone off the hook,
                though.

ROBERT   Why?

OLIVIA   That's what woke me up. Someone phoned.

ROBERT   Tonight?

OLIVIA   Yes, just now. You must have heard it.

ROBERT   The phone? I suppose I did. I thought it was
              on the radio.

OLIVIA   No. A few minutes ago.

ROBERT   Who was it?

OLIVIA   I don't know.

ROBERT   Man or woman?

OLIVIA   I don't know. They hung up.

ROBERT   They hung up?

OLIVIA   Yes.

              (*Pause.*)

OLIVIA   What are you thinking?

ROBERT   Well, let's hope they realised that we're shut
              and now feel quite dreadful about disturbing
              us.

OLIVIA   They were on a mobile I think . . .

ROBERT   Mmm?

OLIVIA   I could hardly hear them, but it's as if their
              signal was bad. And the wind was terrible . . .
              and then . . . and then they just hung up.

ROBERT   Or got cut off more likely.

OLIVIA   Suppose so, yes.

                (*Pause.*)

OLIVIA   They were outside. There's no mobile signal
                around here . . .

ROBERT   None whatsoever.

OLIVIA   . . . Unless you go up into the mountains.
                There's one on Bessy Boot Hill.

ROBERT   So?

OLIVIA   It's blowing a gale out there. Suppose this
                bloke was on Bessy Boot Hill . . .

ROBERT   Come on Liv, don't be silly, no one's going
                to be out in the mountains at this time of
                night and in this weather. You'd have to be
                a madman. Anyway, the wind is blowing
                throughout Britain. It said so on the radio.
                They could just as easily have been on the
                beach in Brighton as be on the side of Bessy
                Boot Hill.

OLIVIA   Yes.

ROBERT   Liv, we came up here to get away from all
                that. No one is looking for you. No one is
                after you.

OLIVIA   I know, I know. I'm fine.

ROBERT   You are. Now come here.

                (*He puts his arm around her again.*)

ROBERT   Nothing will hurt you, not while I'm around.

OLIVIA   Thank you.

                (*Silence. A figure, his face hidden by a
                balaclava appears at the French windows
                and stares in, dimly lit by the light from
                the room. He stares for a moment, unseen.*
                OLIVIA *shivers. The figure moves away.*
                OLIVIA *turns and looks out of the window.*)

ROBERT   Are you all right?

OLIVIA   Can you close the curtains, Robert? I think
                a chill is coming through the windows.

ROBERT   Do it yourself.

OLIVIA   Please?

ROBERT   Fine. (*Gently mocking.*) Anything for you,
                my princess.

OLIVIA   Quite right.

                (*He gets up to close the curtains. One of
                them appears to be stuck on the rail.*)

ROBERT   Bloody hell, the runners are stuck again.

                (*He fiddles with curtains. Nothing happens.
                Suddenly there is a large gust of wind and
                the doors fly open, letting in a howling
                gale.*)

OLIVIA   (*Scream!*)

                (ROBERT, *having been knocked over by the
                left hand door, gets up and shuts them. He
                then goes back to the curtains, this time they
                close. He locks the door.*)

ROBERT	Sorry sweetheart, I went out this afternoon and I must've forgotten to lock the doors.
OLIVIA	(*angrily*) Oh God!
ROBERT	What?
OLIVIA	I hate myself sometimes. Screaming like that. I'm a grown woman, but you must think I'm a little child.
ROBERT	Sometimes. But it's endearing.
OLIVIA	Oh no, how patronising.
ROBERT	But you've also got the sexiest arse in Britain.
OLIVIA	Oh I do, do I?
ROBERT	That arse's the main reason I married you.
	(*He grabs her bottom and pulls her towards him.*)
OLIVIA	Sexist pig.
ROBERT	You weren't complaining earlier.
	(*They laugh softly and embrace. He passes her drink. She finishes it off.*)
ROBERT	Wow, you may be a child sometimes but you don't need any tips on taking your liquor.
OLIVIA	I'm serious though. I hate that still, in the back of my mind . . . there's a little fear left.

ROBERT   I know you won't tell me everything, but
                that old boyfriend of yours has a lot to
                answer for.

OLIVIA   He does.

ROBERT   But if he's as bad as you say he is, the
                likelihood is, he's been banged up in jail.
                He's not coming after you, you must know
                that. He would've done it by now.

OLIVIA   And we're hard to find, aren't we?

ROBERT   Have you looked out of the window lately?
                Sweetheart, we're in the middle of nowhere.
                The only people that find us here are hikers
                who want somewhere to stay a couple of
                nights. Now was this ex of yours a hiker?

OLIVIA   (*laughing at the thought*) No.

ROBERT   No, didn't think he would've been. He's not
                here, he's not on the side of Bessy Boot Hill
                and he's certainly not after you. Not if he
                knows you're married to a tough guy like
                me.

OLIVIA   Oh yes! You, the tough guy. He's the one
                that should be scared.

ROBERT   You betcha!

                (*They laugh.*)

                I'll put some more wood on the fire.

                (ROBERT *puts a log on the fire.* OLIVIA
                *wanders over to the French windows. She
                goes to open the curtains, puts a hand on*

them, then stops herself, takes a sip of the drink and buoyantly . . .)

OLIVIA   Music!

ROBERT   Excuse me?

OLIVIA   Lets have some music!

                (She moves over to the CD player and holds up a CD.)

                This is perfect.

ROBERT   Oh yes?

                (She puts the CD on. "Somethin' Stupid" performed by Frank and Nancy Sinatra begins to play.)

OLIVIA   Dance with me.

ROBERT   Come off it!

OLIVIA   *(playfully)* Robert . . .

ROBERT   Oh, all right then.

                (He gets up and they dance.)

ROBERT   It's nice to think that you regard this as a perfect song for us.

OLIVIA   But it is stupid to say "I love you".

ROBERT   Is it?

OLIVIA   Of course. You're telling me that you've never said it to someone before and immediately regretted it?

ROBERT   I suppose I have.

OLIVIA   I definitely have.

ROBERT   And when you say it to me?

OLIVIA   It's the greatest thing I have ever said and
                my favourite thing to keep saying. I love
                you.

ROBERT   I love you.

OLIVIA   (*both spinning round, laughing*) I love you, I
                love you, I love you!

ROBERT   Whoa . . . okay! We only ate a couple of
                hours ago. It was a very lovely casserole but
                I don't particularly want to see it again.

OLIVIA   (*stopping dancing*) You know I do, truly
                love you Robert, thank you for . . . well . . .
                you know . . .

ROBERT   Yes. I know.

                (*They commence slowly dancing again.*)

                You can tell me anything, Liv.

OLIVIA   Yes.

ROBERT   If there are things, that have, well . . .
                happened, I am here. To listen. Any secrets
                you may have, from the past . . .

OLIVIA   Oh, they're not really secrets . . . they're
                just, things that I wish to forget.

ROBERT   Forget?

OLIVIA	One thing in particular.
ROBERT	Yes?

(*They stop dancing.* OLIVIA, *deep in thought, goes and turns the music off.*)

OLIVIA	It's not like he . . . the thing is . . . he was wonderful.
ROBERT	Wonderful?
OLIVIA	Yes, wonderful. Attractive. He was magnetic and charming. He swept me off my feet. But there was something in him, something – rotten. He did – an awful thing – to someone – something I couldn't believe – All for just . . .
ROBERT	What?
OLIVIA	I made him pay for it.
ROBERT	You? How?
OLIVIA	I . . . I have something, Robert.
ROBERT	Where?
OLIVIA	It's . . . It's . . .
ROBERT	Yes darling?
OLIVIA	Believe me, I wanted to tell you before . . .

(*She stops herself. There is a loud banging at the door. They both jump.*)

ROBERT	Bloody hell! Who'll this be?

(*He makes to answer the door.*)

OLIVIA   Don't answer it. We'll wait for them to go.

ROBERT   But darling . . .

OLIVIA   Shhh.

(*More banging.*)

VOICE   (*calling off*) Hello? Hello? Could I come in?

ROBERT   Do you recognise the voice?

OLIVIA   (*with relief*) No, thank God.

VOICE   (*off*) Er . . . I'm guessing you're shut for the
                winter, but I was wondering if I could have a
                room for the night . . . Just a room. I'm lost
                you see. And rather cold. Hello?

ROBERT   We can't just leave him out there.

OLIVIA   No, I suppose we can't.

(*He goes to the door.*)

ROBERT   If he's a mad axe murderer, I'll politely ask
                him to leave.

OLIVIA   (*deliberately*) Ha-ha.

(*He answers the door. The wind rushes in.*)

ROBERT   (*off*) Come on in.

(*Enter* RAMSAY *followed by* ROBERT. OLIVIA
*visibly relaxes on seeing it's not who she
thought it was.* RAMSAY *is taking off a
balaclava as he comes into the room. He*

*puts it in a jacket pocket. He is a man in his
mid to late thirties, well built and unshaven.
He is dressed for the mountains; wearing
a thick, black hiking jacket, thick woollen
jumper, climbing trousers with zipped
pockets and walking boots.*)

RAMSAY   Bloody freezing out there. I thought I was a
           goner.

ROBERT   Lucky you found us.

RAMSAY   Yes, yes it is, isn't it?

           (*He enters the room further and looks
           around.*)

           Nice place. Lovely.

ROBERT   Thanks.

RAMSAY   You're the owners, are you?

ROBERT   Yes, I'm Robert Chappell and this is my
           wife, Olivia.

RAMSAY   How do you do, Olivia?

OLIVIA   How do you do?

           (*After holding her gaze slightly too long,
           RAMSAY marches over to ROBERT and shakes
           his hand.*)

RAMSAY   Robert, nice to meet you. My name's
           Ramsay.

ROBERT   Nice to meet you, Mr Ramsay.

RAMSAY   No, no. Just Ramsay. So, what do you say?
                You going to put me up for the night?

                (*Pause.* ROBERT *and* OLIVIA *look at each
                other.*)

                I'm almost dead, you know.

OLIVIA   Well, I suppose we could . . .

RAMSAY   Great! Thanks. As you can see I don't have
                any bags, I left them up in the mountains.
                Had to get rid of them, to lose some weight,
                you know. When I realised I was in a spot of
                bother. So, it's just me. Easy really.

ROBERT   Yes.

RAMSAY   I could murder a drink. Any whisky?

ROBERT   Er . . . yes, I'll get you one.

RAMSAY   Large and straight, please.

ROBERT   What?

RAMSAY   The whisky, large, no ice. I've seen enough
                ice to last me a lifetime.

ROBERT   I'm sure.

                (ROBERT *goes to the drinks cabinet and pulls
                out a glass and a bottle of whisky and pours
                a measure. He takes it to* RAMSAY.)

RAMSAY   Cheers.

                (*He downs it, then offers the empty glass to*
                ROBERT.)

May I?

(*Without saying anything, but glancing at his wife*, ROBERT *takes the glass and pours another drink.*)

RAMSAY   It's a Godsend I saw you.

OLIVIA   Saw us?

RAMSAY   I saw your lights on. I could follow them all the way down the mountain. Really put a spring in my step. It was all the better when I found you were a quaint little hotel.

(*He takes the drink from* ROBERT.)

Thanks.

OLIVIA   Yes, well, officially we're closed for the winter.

RAMSAY   Yes, I thought as much. I do quite a bit of winter walking, round here and in Scotland. I find most places shut down for winter.

OLIVIA   No trade, you see.

RAMSAY   Well, you've got me.

OLIVIA   Yes, we do.

RAMSAY   It must happen quite a lot, doesn't it? In winter, I mean. Lost hikers, turning up asking for a room for the night?

ROBERT   We don't really know. This is our first season. We've only owned this place for a few months . . .

RAMSAY   Ah, so I'm you're first waif and stray, am I?
            What an honour. Not that I do it very often
            you understand, crash in on closed hotels.
            I'm a very experienced climber . . . but this
            weather . . . well.

ROBERT   Yes, it's pretty desperate out there.

RAMSAY   I've climbed all over the world, France,
            South America, Tibet, Austria . . . but
            nowhere on earth does the weather come in
            as fast as it does here. One minute bright
            sunshine and singing birds, the next . . .
            this.

            (*There's another gust of wind.*)

ROBERT   How far have you come?

RAMSAY   I came over from Scafell Pike this morning
            then along the top of the valley. A good
            sixteen miles or so. If I'd known the weather
            was going to close in I would have dropped
            down sooner, but I was caught. Saw your
            lights on when I was on . . . Bessy Boot Hill,
            I think it's called.

OLIVIA   Bessy Boot Hill?

RAMSAY   I like the way they call it a hill, quite a
            violent mountain in my opinion. And that
            cliff . . . it falls away into nothingness, for
            hundreds of feet.

ROBERT   Yes, it's been the death of many a climber,
            that cliff.

OLIVIA   Part of it's actually at the bottom of our
            garden.

RAMSAY   Really? (*A thought quickly occurs.*) God,
                you haven't had any casualties dropping
                onto your lawn, have you?

ROBERT   Not yet.

RAMSAY   Good.

                (*Pause.* RAMSAY *takes another large sip of
                his drink, puts the glass down on a small
                table in front of sofa and then walks around
                the room as if inspecting it, watched by the
                other two.*)

RAMSAY   Yes, nice, very nice. Great place for a hotel.

ROBERT   Especially in summer.

RAMSAY   Oh no, in the winter too. Romantic, a bit . . .
                eerie.

OLIVIA   Eerie?

RAMSAY   Yes, don't you think?

OLIVIA   I never thought it eerie.

RAMSAY   Oh I do. Lonely, but romantic.

                (*Pause.* RAMSAY *goes up to the curtains.*)

RAMSAY   The garden you mentioned?

ROBERT   Yes, it goes back quite a long way. We use it
                in the summer. When the weather improves
                we're going to serve dinner out there for the
                guests.

OLIVIA   With the cliff at the bottom it makes for
                quite spectacular surroundings.

RAMSAY   I'm sure.

                (*He looks down at the door handles and
                tries to open the doors. They do not open.*)

RAMSAY   These doors kept locked?

ROBERT   In winter, yes. But we always keep the key
                on the inside.

RAMSAY   Good old health and safety, huh?

ROBERT   Something like that. I only go out that way
                to get firewood. The garden isn't that pretty
                this time of year.

RAMSAY   Uh huh.

                (*He tries the door again then looks out the
                windows. Curtains are still closed.*)

                Right. And you have no other guests?

OLIVIA   No, as we said we're usually . . .

RAMSAY   Closed, yes. It's terribly kind of you to take
                me in like this.

OLIVIA   It's all right, we'd be leaving you to die
                otherwise.

RAMSAY   You would.

OLIVIA   You said you'd dumped your bags on the
                mountain.

RAMSAY   That's right.

OLIVIA   Well, I really don't mean to be rude, but my
                husband and I, we run this place on a very

tight budget and we can't really afford to
have someone staying for free.

RAMSAY   I don't quite understand.

OLIVIA   (*slightly awkward*) Well, I'm sorry, but . . .

ROBERT   I think what my wife is trying to say is that
we'll need paying.

RAMSAY   Oh, I see, you're wondering if I have
my wallet? Yes, didn't leave that on the
mountainside. Always keep certain things
with you.

             (*He reaches into his jacket pocket and pulls
             out a wallet . . .*)

OLIVIA   Not straight away, you understand, I was
just checking . . .

RAMSAY   Here . . .

             (*He pulls out a wad of notes from his
             wallet.*)

RAMSAY   (*continuing*) How's this? Call it an advance
payment. Just in case I do a runner in the
morning.

OLIVIA   Oh that won't be necessary . . .

RAMSAY   Go on. It would make me feel better.

OLIVIA   (*sharing a look with her husband as she
             takes the money*) That's very kind.

RAMSAY   As I said, you've saved my life.

             (*Pause.*)

OLIVIA   If you haven't done a runner, I'll cook you
              breakfast in the morning.

ROBERT   For that price we'll cook you two!

RAMSAY   Sounds wonderful. Thank you.

ROBERT   Can I take your coat?

RAMSAY   Er . . . right. Thanks. Oh, hang on . . .

              (*He takes out a mobile phone, looks at the
              screen.* OLIVIA *notices the phone . . . looks
              at* ROBERT.)

ROBERT   You won't get a signal here, I'm afraid.

RAMSAY   Tell me about it. I got a small signal on
              Bessy Boot Hill, but then I'd saw your lights
              so I thought I'd just climb down here.

              (RAMSAY *puts it in his trouser pocket.*)

OLIVIA   You didn't call us?

RAMSAY   Call you? No. Why?

OLIVIA   No reason.

              (*Pause.*)

ROBERT   Ramsay, your coat?

RAMSAY   Oh, right. Thanks.

              (ROBERT *takes* RAMSAY'S *coat and hangs
              it up on the coat hooks.* RAMSAY *watches
              intensely. There seems to be an awkward
              silence broken by . . .*)

ROBERT   Yes, well . . . I'm sure you'll want to go and
                freshen up, have a shower or something. If
                you don't mind taking Squirrel Nutkin . . .

RAMSAY   I'm sorry?

ROBERT   Squirrel Nutkin. It's the name of the
                room. They're named after Beatrix Potter
                characters.

RAMSAY   How quaint.

ROBERT   My wife's idea, not mine. You'll find it at
                the top of the stairs, to the right. Towels in
                the cupboard.

RAMSAY   And nuts on the bed?

ROBERT   Yes . . . something like that.

RAMSAY   Once again, thanks so much. (*To* OLIVIA.) I
                really am terribly grateful.

                (*He exits upstairs. They give him a moment
                to be out of earshot.*)

ROBERT   He seems nice enough. Slightly odd perhaps,
                but perfectly pleasant.

OLIVIA   Suppose.

ROBERT   And he's certainly taken a liking to you.

OLIVIA   What do you mean?

ROBERT   You know what I mean.

OLIVIA   Oh dear, Robert. Is that a bit of jealousy I'm
                sensing?

ROBERT   Hardly. He's not your type.

OLIVIA   Oh? And what's my type?

ROBERT   Me.

OLIVIA   (*smiling*) I suppose you are.

              (ROBERT *leans in for a kiss. He then moves
              over to the bar. Pause.*)

OLIVIA   I'm not being silly, but don't you think
              . . . there's something about him. An
              atmosphere?

ROBERT   An atmosphere?

OLIVIA   Don't laugh at me, Robert.

ROBERT   No. No I don't think there's an atmosphere
              about him. Anyhow, he's paid us a small
              fortune and I reckon we just get on with
              it. It's easy to be suspicious of every guest
              that comes through the door but it's only
              for one night. Anyhow, he'll be fast asleep
              in five minutes, the night he's had. So
              all we have to do is have another drink,
              relax in front of the fire and fall asleep
              ourselves. Yes?

OLIVIA   Yes.

              (*He collects their glasses and fills them
              up again as* OLIVIA *sits back on the sofa,*
              ROBERT *gives her the drink in her usual
              glass and joins her.* ROBERT *looks up as if
              trying to hear something.*)

OLIVIA   What?

ROBERT   He's probably going through your underwear
              right now.

OLIVIA   (*hitting him with a cushion*) Robert
              Chappell!

              (*They settle back down together cosily, eyes
              shut and drinks in hand. Silence. Gusting
              wind.*)

ROBERT   Before this chap Ramsay arrived, you were
              going to tell me something.

OLIVIA   Was I? That I love you, I expect.

ROBERT   No it wasn't that. You were gonna tell me
              about this boyfriend of yours.

OLIVIA   Sam?

ROBERT   You very rarely call him by his name.

OLIVIA   I don't like to. It makes him seem . . . too
              close.

ROBERT   Sam? Doesn't sound like the name of a
              particularly terrible man.

OLIVIA   You haven't met him.

ROBERT   No, that's true.

OLIVIA   Sam Stone. Stone. That fits.

ROBERT   Does it?

OLIVIA   What his heart is made from. What he
              turned my heart to. Until I met you.

ROBERT   Ah, I'm the stone melter, am I?

OLIVIA   Something like that. I just don't like saying
                his name. It scares me.

ROBERT   There's nothing in a name. Just words.

OLIVIA   And memories.

ROBERT   True. But I'm here to listen to those
                memories. What were you going to tell me,
                earlier?

OLIVIA   I can't remember.

ROBERT   Of course you can.

OLIVIA   Please, Robert, not now.

ROBERT   You really are a funny little fish, aren't you?

OLIVIA   But you understand, don't you?

ROBERT   I suppose I do. So, you won't tell me?

OLIVIA   Not now, no.

                (*Pause.*)

ROBERT   You're going to have to tell me one day.

OLIVIA   Yes. I realise that.

                (*She looks up at him with a real focus.*)

OLIVIA   (*continuing*) Thing is Robert, I know you
                love me. I know how happy I am. So you
                see, I don't want anything to ruin it. I don't
                want you to think badly of me.

ROBERT   Badly of you? Darling, how could I ever . . .

OLIVIA	You could. Anyone can think badly of anyone else. It's human nature.
ROBERT	Perhaps, but I would still love you.
OLIVIA	That's the thing, you would. You may even love me more . . . but for the wrong reasons. Not for the simple, true reasons you love me now. But for other reasons, cheaper, less dignified reasons.
ROBERT	What on earth are you waffling on about?
OLIVIA	I don't know. I'm just . . . Sorry.
ROBERT	Funny little fish.
	(*Pause.* OLIVIA *moves over to* ROBERT.)
ROBERT	One day?
OLIVIA	One day, of course.
ROBERT	Good.
	(*Pause.* OLIVIA *takes* ROBERT'S *hand and gives him a hug and a kiss.*)
OLIVIA	I wonder who he is.
ROBERT	Sorry?
OLIVIA	This Ramsay bloke. I wonder who he is.
ROBERT	Does it matter?
OLIVIA	Of course it matters, he's staying with us.
ROBERT	Darling, we run a hotel, lots of people stay with us.

OLIVIA   Yes, but not like this, when we're shut. We
              don't know anything about him.

ROBERT   What do you want to know?

OLIVIA   I don't know. It's just a feeling I have.

ROBERT   Uh oh, are we into the realms of women's
              intuition?

OLIVIA   A gut feeling. I mean, if you're such an
              experienced climber, do you really get lost
              like that? And what's he doing climbing in
              this weather anyway?

ROBERT   Liv, you're just looking for drama. You
              know as well as I do that climbers get
              caught out all the time, regardless of
              experience. And who was to know the
              weather was going to change so quickly?
              Like he said, it wasn't that bad . . . until a
              few hours ago.

OLIVIA   But aren't you the slightest bit interested?

ROBERT   Not really, I just want him to fall asleep and
              leave when he wakes up. He's paid us. That's
              all that matters.

              (*He sits down and holds her once again.
              Silence. From behind the curtains . . .
              there's a sharp knocking at the windows.
              They both jump.*)

OLIVIA   What was that?

ROBERT   Shhh . . .

              (*Nothing is heard except for the wind.*)

It was just the wind.

OLIVIA   The wind?

ROBERT   A branch . . . blown against a window.

OLIVIA   You think so?

ROBERT   Yes.

OLIVIA   Gave me a hell of a shock.

                (*She gets up, yawns and stretches then looks briefly at the window. She goes over to the CDs and starts looking through them, as if planning the next piece of music.* ROBERT *remains, eyes closed again, hands behind his head. Silence. More knocking at the window.* OLIVIA *drops some CDs.*)

ROBERT   (*getting up*) Bloody hell!

                (*Pause.*)

OLIVIA   (*making towards the window*) Well, if you're not going to look I . . .

ROBERT   All right, fine!

                (*He makes towards the window . . . More knocking, louder and quicker this time . . .*)

ROBERT   What the hell?

                (ROBERT *goes to the curtains, he puts his hands on them . . . and as quickly as possible draws them back. There is nothing but darkness.*)

ROBERT   *(with relieved chuckling turning away from the window)* There's nothing there darling, look.

OLIVIA   But the knocking?

ROBERT   The weather, playing tricks. If it wasn't a branch, then it could have been the shed door banging in the wind, that's all.

OLIVIA   Will you have a look?

ROBERT   Outside? Oh come off it, Liv . . .

OLIVIA   It'll only take a few seconds.

ROBERT   Oh God . . . all right.

                (He slips the boots on, unlocks and opens the French windows.)

OLIVIA   Take this.

                (She hands him the poker from next to the stove.)

ROBERT   What the hell's that for?

OLIVIA   Just take it.

ROBERT   Fine. I'll be two minutes.

                (ROBERT steps outside, feeling the cold. He turns to his right and walks out of view. OLIVIA follows him with her gaze from the threshold of the door, hugging herself for warmth. A strong gust of wind. The lights flicker . . . She starts, turns around and re-enters the room slightly to see what's going on.)

OLIVIA   Ramsay? Hello?

          (OLIVIA *goes back to the windows and steps*
          outside again.)

          Robert! Robert I can't see you! Where are
          you?

          (*She turns and looks the opposite way (SR)*
          with her back to where ROBERT *went.*)

          Robert, please!

          (*Suddenly,* ROBERT *jumps out from behind*
          her with a roar.)

OLIVIA   (*Scream!*)

          (ROBERT *laughs, holding the poker in one*
          hand and a branch in the other.)

          You bastard! You complete and utter
          bastard! That's not funny, that's not funny at
          all.

ROBERT   I'm sorry sweetheart, I'm sorry. Look . . .

          (*He shows her the branch.*)

          There are hundreds of these blowing about.

          (ROBERT *throws the branch out through the*
          French window.)

ROBERT   (*continuing*) It just takes one to rattle
          against a window and you hear what we
          heard.

          (*He shuts the French windows.*)

Nothing more sinister than a branch.

OLIVIA   I just wanted to be sure, that's all.

              (ROBERT *moves down to fireplace and*
              replaces the poker. Enter RAMSAY *quickly,*
              from the bedrooms.)

RAMSAY   Is everything all right? I thought I heard
              shouting.

ROBERT   Everything's fine thanks, Ramsay, just a
              little joke, that's all.

OLIVIA   It was not a joke. It was . . . well, it wasn't
              funny.

ROBERT   No it wasn't funny.

RAMSAY   Thank goodness, I was just getting out of
              the shower when I heard it.

ROBERT   Do you feel revived?

RAMSAY   I do, thanks. A torrent of hot water in
              Squirrel Nutkin's bathroom has made me
              feel like a new man.

ROBERT   Good.

RAMSAY   Do you mind if I join you down here? Better
              than sitting upstairs on my own.

OLIVIA   Oh . . . of course.

RAMSAY   Thanks, it's nice to have company.

ROBERT   Yes . . . (*Indicating the chairs.*) please.

(RAMSAY *walks to the sofa and is about to sit down . . .*)

Would you like another whisky?

RAMSAY   That would be wonderful, thanks.

(*He picks up* OLIVIA'S *glass from the coffee table.*)

I think this is my glass isn't it?

OLIVIA   No, that's mine.

(*She takes it from him.*)

Your glass is here.

(*She picks up his glass and hands it to him.*)

There's a little left.

RAMSAY   Oh, that's not like me.

(*He takes the glass whilst keeping his eyes on* OLIVIA *and finishes off the drink and hands it back to her.*)

OLIVIA   I'll get you another one.

(*She puts her own glass on top of the drinks cabinet and pours him another drink then hands it to him.*)

RAMSAY   You can tell the windows have been open in here.

OLIVIA   Why?

RAMSAY   It's like an ice box.

ROBERT   I'll just put some more wood on the fire.
              (*Seeing the empty log basket.*) Ah, I'll go
              and get some more from the shed.

              (OLIVIA *hands the drink to* RAMSAY.)

RAMSAY   Thanks.

              (ROBERT *picks up the small wood basket
              from next to the stove, moves up to the
              French windows, puts his boots back on and
              opens French windows.*)

RAMSAY   I can go if you like?

ROBERT   No. You stay where you are and have your
              drink. I'll only be a few minutes. Ta-ta for
              now.

              (ROBERT *exits, shutting the windows behind
              him. Awkward silence.* RAMSAY *takes a few
              tentative sips from his glass.* OLIVIA *still
              by the windows looking out after* ROBERT.
              Pause.)

RAMSAY   Now, you either love me, or you hate me.

              (OLIVIA *turns towards* RAMSAY.)

OLIVIA   I'm sorry?

RAMSAY   I said, you either love me or you hate me.

OLIVIA   I don't know what you're getting at.

RAMSAY   It's the atmosphere you're creating. I can
              feel it. You're either head over heels in love
              with me or you hate me.

OLIVIA   Well, I can assure I don't love you.

(OLIVIA *moves over to the chair and sits down*.)

RAMSAY   Ah, so you hate me.

OLIVIA   No. No, I don't hate you.

RAMSAY   You don't?

OLIVIA   No, of course not. I mean, I may be a little, nervous in your presence, but I don't hate you.

RAMSAY   Nervous?

OLIVIA   Yes.

RAMSAY   Why?

OLIVIA   Oh, I don't know. It's not just you, it's been an odd evening all round. Lots of strange things have happened. Strange noises and . . . strange phone calls . . .

RAMSAY   Strange phone calls?

OLIVIA   Yes. From a mobile.

RAMSAY   Oh, I see, and you think it's me. Well, I can assure you I've not made any phone calls. Not to here, not to anywhere. You're very beautiful, you know that?

OLIVIA   What?

RAMSAY   I said, you're very beautiful.

(OLIVIA *shifts in her chair*.)

RAMSAY   I'm just making conversation. Paying a
           compliment.

OLIVIA   Well, thank you. I suppose.

RAMSAY   Not at all.

           (RAMSAY *moves up to the drinks cabinet for
           a re-fill.*)

           You know, finding this place . . . when I was
           on the mountainside, in a freezing blizzard,
           a howling gale . . . thinking that I was . . .
           well . . . then I saw the lights on here. In the
           distance. This charming little place, with
           such hospitable hosts . . . well, it was like
           finding . . . a diamond in the rough.

OLIVIA   (*she darts him a look*) What did you say?

RAMSAY   I said; it was like finding a diamond in the
           rough. Don't you think?

OLIVIA   I . . . I don't know.

RAMSAY   Oh, I'm sure you do.

           (*They hold each other's gaze.* OLIVIA *leaps
           out of the chair and moves over to the
           French windows.*)

OLIVIA   Where's Robert? He's been ages.

RAMSAY   Gathering firewood can take a while.

OLIVIA   He only had that little basket to fill.

RAMSAY   Well, he had to chop it, didn't he?

OLIVIA   No, we chopped it during the summer.

RAMSAY	Well, there's no need to panic, I'm sure there's a perfectly simple explanation.
OLIVIA	I can't see the shed light on. You can usually see the glow of the light. Why isn't it on?
RAMSAY	Now, don't worry.
OLIVIA	(*turning on him slowly*) You said you'd had a shower . . .
RAMSAY	What?
OLIVIA	(*backing away from him*) You said you'd had a shower!
RAMSAY	That's right, I did.
OLIVIA	Why are you here?
RAMSAY	I don't know what's got into you . . .
OLIVIA	You said you were in the shower. You said you heard a scream, then you rushed downstairs to see if everything was all right.
RAMSAY	Yes, I did. Look, are you okay? I . . .
OLIVIA	Your hair!
RAMSAY	What the hell are you talking about?
OLIVIA	Your hair is dry and all your clothes look exactly the same. You didn't have a shower . . . you were lying. You were somewhere else. Robert! Robert!
RAMSAY	For God's sake, Olivia!
OLIVIA	Who are you? Did he send you?

RAMSAY   What? Listen, I need you to calm down . . .

OLIVIA   A diamond in the rough? He's sent you!

RAMSAY   Olivia, calm down . . .

OLIVIA   He's sent you, I know he has!

RAMSAY   I haven't a clue what you're talking about!

OLIVIA   Robert! Robert!

                (ROBERT *throws the doors open and enters
                carrying the filled log basket.*)

ROBERT   What the bloody hell's going on?

OLIVIA   Robert, where were you?

ROBERT   (*holding up the log basket*) Getting
                firewood. I told you. The light in the shed
                has gone, I couldn't see what I was doing . . .
                it took ages. Sorry sweetheart. Now, calm
                down, just calm down.

                (ROBERT *takes his boots off and puts his
                slippers on.*)

RAMSAY   I'm sorry, I don't know what I did. I was just
                chatting and . . .

ROBERT   It's all right Ramsay, she can get like this
                sometimes.

OLIVIA   Don't talk about me as if I'm mad, as if I'm
                not here! I'm not crazy. He's here for me.
                He's here to get it from me.

RAMSAY   I assure you, I don't know what she's talking
                about.

(RAMSAY *takes the log basket from* ROBERT *and moves down to the stove and puts some wood on the fire.*)

ROBERT   No, I'm sure. Listen, darling, I'll pour you a drink, then perhaps you should go to bed.

OLIVIA   I don't want to go to bed. Not with him in the house!

ROBERT   (*grabbing her, angrily*) Now listen! Don't be so damned stupid! Pull yourself together . . . It's embarrassing . . . Now just sit down and I'll get you a drink.

                (*He puts her onto the sofa then shuts the French windows.*)

                I'm sorry about this, Ramsay.

RAMSAY   That's quite all right, perhaps I should go to bed.

ROBERT   You'll do no such thing. As I said, you're our guest and you'll stay here and relax. She'll pull herself together in a bit.

                (*He pours* OLIVIA *a straight gin, not in her usual glass.*)

                There you go, sweetheart.

OLIVIA   That's not my glass.

ROBERT   You'll make do with that one. You've got to drop these silly obsessions you have. Just have that and go to bed.

OLIVIA   Stop ordering me around like a child.

ROBERT   Then stop behaving like one!

                (OLIVIA *takes the glass from* ROBERT.)

                Now, Ramsay, may I top up your glass?

RAMSAY   Er . . . yes, thank you very much.

ROBERT   Please, sit down and relax.

RAMSAY   Are you sure? I don't want to . . .

ROBERT   Please.

RAMSAY   Okay. Thanks.

                (*He sits down on the sofa next to* OLIVIA
                ROBERT *pours him a drink in his usual glass
                and hands it to him.*)

                Thanks very much.

ROBERT   I'll join you, I think.

                (*He looks for a glass and finds* OLIVIA'S. *He
                pours a whisky into it.*)

ROBERT   I'm not usually a whisky man, but on a night
                like this, well, it warms you up, doesn't it?

RAMSAY   It certainly does.

ROBERT   So cold. I can't feel my hands after bringing
                the firewood in. There you go Liv . . . a nice
                fire, to warm you up.

OLIVIA   Robert, don't patronise me.

ROBERT   Are you going to drink that?

OLIVIA	There's no tonic in it . . . I hate straight gin.
ROBERT	It'll do you good, just have it.
	(OLIVIA *takes a small sip of her drink and grimaces.*)
ROBERT	There you go.
	(*He smiles and takes a sip of his own drink.*)
OLIVIA	You're using my glass.
ROBERT	Oh, don't be silly Olivia. (*With a sigh.*) May I please use your glass?
OLIVIA	Yes.
ROBERT	Thank you. (*To* RAMSAY.) This is her favourite glass, given to her by her mother before she died.
OLIVIA	It's one of the few things I have left of her.
RAMSAY	How lovely. I have a similar thing. From my mother and father.
ROBERT	You've lost your parents?
RAMSAY	Afraid so. My mother died when I was a child, my father just over a year ago.
ROBERT	I'm sorry.
RAMSAY	Yes, lots of people are sorry. He was a dearly loved man. Shouldn't have died the way he did.
OLIVIA	How did he die?

RAMSAY   (*matter of fact*) Unnaturally.

                (*Pause.*)

                Or rather . . . without warning.

OLIVIA   That must have been very . . .

RAMSAY   Shocking?

OLIVIA   Yes . . . shocking. Very shocking.

RAMSAY   It was.

ROBERT   I'm sure. Not that we want to dwell . . .

RAMSAY   The crazy thing is; that's all I feel. Shock.
                And anger. When it comes like that, when
                you're not expecting it . . . you never . . . I
                have never really had any time to grieve.

OLIVIA   You must make the time. I had to.

RAMSAY   Did you? Yes, I suppose I must.

                (*A beat.*)

RAMSAY   He was a wonderful man.

                (*He takes a sip of his drink. Silence.
                Awkward.* ROBERT *downs the rest of his
                drink.*)

ROBERT   (*trying to lighten the atmosphere*) So
                Ramsay, what do you do for a living?

RAMSAY   Ah, this is where I get embarrassed.

ROBERT   Really? Why?

RAMSAY	Well, you see I don't do much at all. Not for a living anyway.
ROBERT	Oh, really?
OLIVIA	Isn't that a little boring?
RAMSAY	Not at all. Getting lost, for example, can be very exhilarating.
OLIVIA	But, generally, isn't it a little dull, not to have anything to do?
RAMSAY	Oh, since father died, I've had a great deal to do, I've not been at all bored.
ROBERT	I see. A nice position to be in. A man of leisure.
RAMSAY	I'd rather have my father back.
ROBERT	Of course . . . yes. I didn't mean to . . . you know.
RAMSAY	Uh huh.
	(*Pause.*)
ROBERT	Darling, you look tired. Do you think we should go to bed?
	(ROBERT *moves over to* OLIVIA *and takes her glass.*)
OLIVIA	Yes, I think I am quite tired.
	(*She gets up.*)
ROBERT	Come on then, sweetheart.

(*Beat.*)

ROBERT   Right then . . .

(ROBERT *puts* OLIVIA'S *and his own glass on top of the drinks cabinet. He then closes the curtains of French windows.*)

RAMSAY   I'm sorry, I didn't mean to make you feel uncomfortable.

ROBERT   No, of course not . . . we understand. Feel free to stay down here if you want. Have another drink.

RAMSAY   Thanks. Seems a shame to waste such a lovely fire.

ROBERT   I'll just make it a little cosier for you.

(ROBERT *turns out the main light; the room is dimly lit from wall lights and fireplace.*)

RAMSAY   A home from home.

ROBERT   Well, goodnight then.

RAMSAY   Goodnight. Goodnight Olivia.

OLIVIA   Goodnight.

(ROBERT *and* OLIVIA *exit upstairs.* RAMSAY, *looking at the door, gives them a few moments, puts his unfinished glass of whisky on the coffee table. He checks that they have gone. Then he:*

- *moves over to the reception desk*
- *gets the cash box out*
- *takes out the money and looks inside*

*- puts the money back and puts the money
box back*
- looks behind notice board
- moves over to the bar, searching
- moves down to the stove and look around

ROBERT *appears, unseen, at the top of the
stairs to the bedrooms. He observes* RAMSAY
searching for something.

RAMSAY *moves over to the mirror and looks
behind it. He then quickly goes to his jacket
that is hanging in hallway.* RAMSAY *unzips
a pocket and takes out a jewellery case. He
opens the case and produces a necklace. This
necklace has a centrepiece with a good sized
ruby on the right and sapphire on the left of
equal size. In the middle there is a gap, as if
a stone were missing. He places the necklace
in a trouser pocket and zips it up.*

ROBERT *watches* RAMSAY *as he places the
empty jewellery case back in his jacket and
zips it closed.*

RAMSAY *moves upstage with his back
towards the French windows.* ROBERT *makes
sure that he remains out of sight at all
times.* RAMSAY *stands in front of the French
windows . . .*

*We hear nothing but the whistling of the
wind.*

Silence.

Then suddenly . . .

*Through the French windows bursts a
figure holding a climbing rope, he leaps*

onto RAMSAY, *slipping the rope around
his neck and starts to strangle him. The
two figures tumble around the room for a
few moments, bashing into the walls and
furniture, until* RAMSAY, *fighting for breath
loses his strength and is overpowered by the
masked figure. They end up centre stage, as*
RAMSAY *drops to his knees choking and then
eventually his whole body is lowered onto
the floor, dead. The figure in a balaclava
stands over the corpse.*

ROBERT, *still on the stairs, steps into the
room.*)

OLIVIA   (*off*) Robert? Robert?

(ROBERT *surveys the scene as* OLIVIA *comes
rushing in, seeing the scene before her.*)

OLIVIA   (*Scream!)*

*The figure drops the rope and turns to them
both. He walks over to the glass of whisky
that* RAMSAY *was drinking and then takes off
the balaclava revealing a handsome man.
This is* SAM STONE.)

SAM   Hello Liv.

OLIVIA   Sam? No . . . Please God, no.

(*She holds* ROBERT.)

SAM   (*coolly*) Is that all the thanks I get? And
                to think I've just saved your life. I think I
                deserve this . . . cheers.

(*He grins and takes a sip of whisky.*)

END OF ACT ONE

ACT TWO

As before . . .

SAM   Well? Come on . . . where's the hug? The
           heroes welcome? The kiss?

ROBERT   What the f . . . ?

SAM   . . . Liv, introduce me. You're not playing
           the dignified hostess very well. (*After a
           beat, to* ROBERT.) Sam Stone, Liv may have
           told you about me.

OLIVIA   Please Sam . . . please, just . . .

SAM   Just what?

OLIVIA   Please Sam, leave us alone.

SAM   Leave you alone! My God . . . I've just
           travelled all the way from London to save
           your life, and you want me to leave you
           alone? Now, I don't know about you, but that
           seems a little ungrateful to me.

OLIVIA   How did you . . .

SAM   How did I find you? Liv, I always knew
           where you were. You don't think I'd just let
           the love of my life disappear did you?

ROBERT   Love of your life? Don't talk rubbish. You
           tore her life apart.

SAM   Who the hell are you? Standing there
           dressed like Englebert Humperdink, holding
           onto to my girl . . . I've a good mind to kill
           you too.

ROBERT   I'm Robert Chappell.

SAM   Robert Chappell? Oh! So this is the new
              husband is it, Liv? The 'one'. 'Til death do
              you part and all that.

OLIVIA   How do you know I'm married?

SAM   I've kept a close eye on you. So, you've gone
              and married this knitwear model. Are you
              pregnant? Was it a shotgun?

ROBERT   How dare you.

              (*Pause.*)

SAM   Aren't you the cat that's got the cream, eh,
              Bobby?

ROBERT   Robert.

SAM   Well, congratulations! Congratu-bloody-
              lations! You could've at least invited me. I
              love a good wedding. Was it a big do?

ROBERT   We're not telling you anything.

SAM   You know, I've only been here two minutes
              and you're already starting to really piss
              me off. I would be more cordial if I were
              you, how many corpses do you want in your
              living room?

ROBERT   I'm phoning the police.

SAM   Not a good idea.

              (*He takes out a gun.*)

OLIVIA   Oh, please, no . . .

SAM	Really, not a good idea.
	(ROBERT *has the telephone to his ear, he stops.*)
SAM	I'm not the bad guy here, he is. Luckily, the bad guy's dead.
ROBERT	How's he the bad guy?
SAM	Oh, didn't I tell you? About an hour and a half ago, that man tried to kill me.
ROBERT	Ramsay?
SAM	If that's his real name, yes. Ramsay tried to kill me. He should be more thorough next time.
ROBERT	I don't believe you.
SAM	Of course you don't, because you don't want to believe me. Because Liv will have filled your head with stories about how evil, how destructive I am, how I ruined her life and you want me to be the bad guy. You know nothing about me, so don't start judging me on the basis of the ramblings of a half-mad cow like her!
ROBERT	You speak about my wife like that again and I'll . . .
SAM	Yes, yes, yes, you'll kill me. Only make threats like that when you too have a gun in your hand Bobby. I'm a tolerant kind of fella but I don't take kindly to lap-dog husbands trying to play the hero.
ROBERT	That gun's not even loaded.

SAM   Excuse me?

ROBERT   I don't believe that the gun is loaded.

SAM   Oh dear, you're really coming across as a bit
           of a fool. Why the hell would I be carrying a
           gun that wasn't loaded?

OLIVIA   Robert, trust me . . . it will be loaded.

SAM   Listen to your wife.

ROBERT   But if it was loaded, why would he have
           strangled Ramsay? You could have shot him.

SAM   Thank you Poirot, but you're not thinking.
           Not using those little grey cells. I didn't
           shoot him, because none of us want a
           murder investigation do we? No. Now, there
           would definitely be one if he was found with
           a bullet in his back. But now, because I was
           thinking straight, we can move his body, put
           it at the bottom of the cliff of Bessy Boot
           Hill and in a few days, when this weather
           has cleared, mountain rescue will find him
           and decide that he had a climbing accident.
           It's pretty simple, if you have the right sort
           of brain.

ROBERT   I'm glad I don't have that sort of brain.

SAM   Me too, otherwise you may be a trickier
           prospect to deal with.

           (SAM *gathers the rope up from around the
           body and hands it to* ROBERT.)

           Right. Take this . . . And take the body to
           the bottom of the cliff. It won't take long;
           it's only at the bottom of your garden. Wrap

the rope up all around him. The trick is, to
make it look like he fell, got tangled up in
the rope, and died of exposure or accidently
strangled himself. Make it artistic.

ROBERT   Why the hell should I?

SAM   Why should you? Two reasons. One, you
don't want a body found in your living
room. And two, this gun is loaded. Now, any
more questions? Good, move the body. Now!

(SAM *moves up to the French windows and
opens them.*)

OLIVIA   It's best we do exactly as he says, you know.

ROBERT   I'll be back as soon as I can.

(ROBERT *puts his coat on.*)

ROBERT   I'm not scared of him.

SAM   Yes, you are.

OLIVIA   I love you.

ROBERT   I love you too.

(SAM *raises he eyes to the sky.* ROBERT *goes
over to the body and is about to try and pick
him up.*)

ROBERT   Can you give me a hand?

SAM   Not likely. But you're learning, trying to
get me off my guard. Good. You look like
a fit enough sort of bloke, just get him
outside and stick him in a wheelbarrow or
something.

ROBERT   You have no scruples, do you?

SAM   Blame my parents . . .

            (ROBERT *grabs the body under the arms and
            drags it to the French windows.* ROBERT *exits
            with the body.*)

SAM   Au revoir, Bobby.

ROBERT   Robert.

            (ROBERT *is seen outside the French windows
            dragging the body, turning right with the
            body, out of view.* SAM *shuts the doors.*)

SAM   So, how's my little schnuffle face?

OLIVIA   Don't call me that.

            (*Pause.*)

SAM   Are you going to sit down? You're making
            me nervous.

OLIVIA   That'll be a first.

SAM   Come and sit down.

            (*She does so, very hesitantly.*)

            Can I get you a drink?

OLIVIA   No thanks.

SAM   Oh, come on, Liv, are you going to be like
            this all night? I expected a bit of a warmer
            welcome.

OLIVIA   Then you were very much mistaken.

SAM   It's great to see you.

            (*He gets no response.*)

            How have you been doing?

OLIVIA   Very well. Wonderfully in fact. I knew it
            would be ruined, I just knew it.

SAM   Ruined?

OLIVIA   You would never leave me alone. I could
            feel it.

SAM   (*going to stroke her face*) Of course I was
            never going to leave you alone. You made
            sure of that.

OLIVIA   Don't touch me.

SAM   Why not?

OLIVIA   Not with those hands.

SAM   Oh don't be so melodramatic, Olivia. Relax,
            it's not as if we're strangers.

OLIVIA   Oh, but we are, Sam. I don't know you.

SAM   You're having fun really. You like this.

OLIVIA   You have no idea how much I hate this. How
            much I hate . . .

SAM   Don't say it, don't you dare say it! You don't
            hate me, I can see it in your eyes, you don't
            hate me at all. You knew one day I'd find
            you, that I'd come back. You guaranteed
            that. And now I'm here I've spiced up your
            life once again. Made it . . . exciting.

OLIVIA   I don't want an exciting life. I like my quiet,
             normal life, the one I've been living. And
             now you've come and wrecked it. Bulldozed
             in and destroyed all that I've grown to love.

SAM   You were bored, weren't you? Until this,
             until tonight, you were bored. I bet . . . well,
             how many times have you been turned on
             since you left me? None, not properly. That's
             my guess.

OLIVIA   Then you guess wrong.

SAM   Living in the back end of nowhere with that
             boring husband of yours . . .

OLIVIA   He's far from boring.

SAM   Well, no offence to your new spouse, but he
             hardly oozes excitement.

OLIVIA   He oozes love, which is more than can be
             said for you.

SAM   I loved you, I looked after you, I made you
             feel alive. And you threw it all in my face.
             Betrayed me and stole from me.

OLIVIA   You deserved it!

             (*Pause.*)

SAM   I still love you, Olivia.

OLIVIA   Liar.

SAM   I loved you from the moment I saw you in
             that pokey restaurant. Remember that day?
             I've always loved you and I'll love you until
             the day I die.

OLIVIA	I'm not listening.
SAM	If I didn't love you, do you think I would have let you get away with what you've done? Do you think I would've just let you go? I knew that one day you'd come back to me.
OLIVIA	You've come back to *me*.
SAM	True, but only because I've run out of patience. You can't spend too long torturing yourself, too long wanting something and missing something so desperately that your life is not the same without it.
OLIVIA	Are you talking about missing me . . . or the diamond? Don't insult my intelligence Sam. I know that's why you're here.
SAM	I'm here to claim what is rightfully mine.
OLIVIA	Rightfully yours? You killed a man to get it!
SAM	I was talking about you.
OLIVIA	Neither are yours. I hate to burst this egotistic bubble that you're living in, but they're not.
SAM	Don't say stupid things, Olivia.
OLIVIA	I'm a married woman. I'm Robert's. Not yours. I am Mrs Olivia Chappell.
	(*Pause.*)
	What's the matter, Sam? Can't stand losing things, can you? Can't stand to think that

someone has outdone you. Not something
you're used to is it?

SAM   I haven't lost anything. You're still in love
with me and you've still got the diamond.

OLIVIA   It's not yours.

SAM   Where is it, Olivia?

OLIVIA   You'll have to kill me first.

SAM   Believe me I will. It'll hurt me, but I will.
Where is it?

OLIVIA   Why, Sam? Why now? You could have come
at any time. You said you knew where I was.

SAM   Of course I did. And I knew that wherever
you were, the diamond was going to be. So,
as far as I could see, for the months or years
it took for all the fuss about the theft to die
down, it was in safe keeping.

OLIVIA   You still have the rest of the necklace, you
still have a ruby and a sapphire . . . you did
pretty well.

SAM   You know as well as I do that without
the diamond the necklace is as good as
worthless. That's why you took it. It was a
shrewd move. So where is it?

OLIVIA   There's no point threatening me. I'm the one
in control.

SAM   Don't kid yourself.

OLIVIA   You haven't answered my question, why
now?

SAM   We, have a buyer.

OLIVIA   You're joking.

SAM   No.

OLIVIA   But you thought it would take years before
               you could safely sell that necklace.

SAM   The heat has died down, it's been over a
               year now and anyway, the price is right.
               With the diamond that is.

OLIVIA   Who is it?

SAM   I'm not going to tell you that.

OLIVIA   I'm the one who knows where the diamond
               is, Sam.

               (*Pause.*)

SAM   To tell you the truth, I don't know. Not
               exactly. Only a name; Victor. He contacted
               me a few weeks ago. Said he was interested
               in the necklace and offered a good price. A
               great price. Said he would do anything to
               get their hands on it. Some sort of collector,
               in Paris.

OLIVIA   Paris?

SAM   Yeah. A collector of Napoleonic artefacts.
               He'd tracked me down. He said he was going
               to send a middle man round, a go between.
               Who visited me a few days later. He asked
               to see the necklace before handing over any
               money. Of course. He wasn't best pleased
               when he had to tell his boss that the most
               valuable colour was missing. The Tricolour

necklace, once the property of Napoleon
Bonaparte himself . . . was only a deux
couleur.

OLIVIA   I can imagine.

SAM   I told him I'd split the stones for security but
             I knew where the diamond was and I'd get
             it. You see, I've got friends the length and
             breadth of this country, Liv. A few calls, a
             few favours owed and it was easy to follow
             your progress. I found out you'd come north
             and married some bloke called Chappell.
             Then it was easy to find a quaint little hotel
             in the Lake District being run by none other
             . . . than you.

OLIVIA   You'd tracked me, all this time?

SAM   Of course I tracked you. But as I said, it sort
             of worked, it was a security policy . . . only
             the two of us knew where the final piece of
             the necklace was. I said I'd come and get the
             diamond but Victor insisted on sending this
             bloke, the go between, with me.

OLIVIA   Why?

SAM   As a witness, to check I wasn't lying and to
             validate the diamond before any money was
             handed over.

OLIVIA   Where's this go-between now?

SAM   Well, if your Hubby's done his job correctly
             . . . he should be lying at the foot of the cliff
             of Bessy Boot Hill.

OLIVIA   What? Ramsay?

SAM	He tried to kill me, Liv. Up on the mountain. We didn't know the weather was going to be this bad. About fifteen miles from here the car got stuck, we couldn't get through. So, we walked. We had the right equipment because the plan was to put Ramsay in here posing as a climber, he couldn't just turn up in a three piece suit carrying a briefcase. So, we started the hike, it was hard going but at least I knew where we were headed. Then, just as we saw the lights of this place and he could find his way without me, he attacked me, knocked me out and left me for dead. He did what I did to him. Only, without success. I woke up about an hour later . . . he'd stolen the necklace from me and made his way down here. I used my mobile and phoned . . .
OLIVIA	It was you?
SAM	. . . He'd come to steal the diamond, complete the necklace and have it for himself. Ramsay was going to kill you, Liv, if he couldn't find the diamond. I have no doubt he would have killed you both.
OLIVIA	I don't believe you.
SAM	Yes you do. Know why? Because I'll bet you could sense it. You always were good at judging people. I bet you could tell there was something, not quite right, the moment he entered the room.
	(*Pause.*)
SAM	Of course you did.
OLIVIA	But this bloke, Victor, he's not going to buy it now, surely?

SAM   Why not? He doesn't care if anyone is killed
             as long as he gets what he wants. All I have
             to do is explain there was an accident but
             that the necklace is safe . . . the deal will
             still be on.

OLIVIA   So you were just planning on arriving here,
             asking me for the diamond and buggering
             off?

SAM   Of course not. Remember what I told you
             once . . . that I would get you the most
             beautiful necklace in the world. To show
             how much I loved you. This necklace, it's
             ours. And the money will be ours too.

OLIVIA   You're living in a dream world.

             (*Pause.*)

             Oh Sam. You were always just a petty crook.
             A loveable rogue. With a gun in your pocket
             you'd never use.

SAM   I'm still him, schnuffle face.

OLIVIA   No. No, not now. You've gone too far. You're
             out of your depth. The moment you killed a
             man to steal that necklace was the moment
             you became someone else. And now you're
             here, having killed again and striking deals
             with Parisian gangsters! It's madness, I saw
             it, a year ago, I saw it in your eyes, you'd
             changed. That's why I couldn't let you get
             away with it. That's why I ran away with the
             diamond. You should never have given it to
             me to look after.

SAM   I trusted you.

OLIVIA   And I you.

          (*Pause.*)

SAM   You could've just called the police.

OLIVIA   I suppose I should have done, yes. But I
          couldn't, I still loved you Sam. I hated you
          for what you'd done, but I still loved you. I
          ran off with the diamond to hurt you.

SAM   You ran off with it to guarantee you'd see
          me again.

OLIVIA   No. You having an incomplete necklace,
          seeing it every day, was far more torturous
          than having no necklace at all.

SAM   And to think, I did it all for you.

OLIVIA   For me? There's nothing romantic about
          what you did! You messed up stealing a
          necklace from some aristocrat. It was all
          over the news, how it had gone wrong . . .
          even you admitted that you didn't want to
          kill anyone.

SAM   Messed it up? The police never caught me!

OLIVIA   We had to go into hiding! I had to leave
          everything behind . . . my friends, my home
          . . . it was never meant to be like that, Sam.
          You were never that sort of guy.

SAM   I was trying to give you the life you
          deserved.

OLIVIA   You ruined my life! You killed a man!

SAM   An old man! I killed an old man! Poor sod
               was dying anyway, couldn't go anywhere
               without an oxygen mask attached to his
               face. I only did what nature would have
               done a few weeks later. He wasn't supposed
               to be there, Liv.

OLIVIA   Old or not, dying or not . . . it doesn't
               excuse it.

SAM   Perhaps not . . . but it makes it slightly
               easier to live with, doesn't it? Slightly more
               . . . palatable. I still love you schnuffle face.

OLIVIA   Don't call me that.

SAM   But I do.

               (Pause. She is being won over.)

               I would do anything for you . . . I would lay
               down my own life. For you. Wouldn't I? You
               wanted to see me again, Liv. That's why you
               took the diamond, so I would come and find
               you. One day. You may have wanted to leave
               me then, but not forever. And here I am,
               back with you, where you want me to be.

               (He turns her towards himself.)

               Look at me. I love you more than life itself.
               And you still love me.

               (He kisses her.)

OLIVIA   Yes. Yes I do.

               (ROBERT appears at the window.)

SAM	Now, let's get that diamond and make some serious money.
	(*They kiss again.* ROBERT *opens the French windows and enters.*)
ROBERT	What the bloody hell is going on?
SAM	Sorry Bobby, seems Liv and I had some unfinished business.
ROBERT	(*to* SAM.) You bastard!
	(*He attacks* SAM, *trying to get the gun from him. In the melee the gun slides out and* OLIVIA *picks it up. The fight comes to a close as* SAM *overpowers* ROBERT.)
SAM	Good girl, Liv, good girl. Give me the gun.
	(*She keeps hold of it.*)
	Give me the gun, Olivia.
OLIVIA	No.
	(*She points it at* SAM.)
	Get in the chair. Now.
	(*She ushers him with the barrel of the gun to the chair.*)
SAM	Oh dear . . . you're making a huge mistake.
OLIVIA	No, I made that mistake years ago when I let you into my life.
SAM	Harsh.

OLIVIA

But true. Love you? I can't stand to look at you, to breathe the same air as you! Did you really think you could just burst back into my life and sell me a pack of lies?

SAM

I haven't lied, everything I told you was the truth.

OLIVIA

Truth? You don't know the meaning of the word.

SAM

Come off it, Liv. You know as well as I do that I wouldn't lie about this.

ROBERT

Lie about what?

OLIVIA

Later.

ROBERT

Olivia . . .

OLIVIA

Go and get something to tie his hands with.

ROBERT

I'm not sure that's a good idea . . .

OLIVIA

Just get some rope from the shed.

(ROBERT *goes to the French windows, exits and closes them after himself.*)

SAM

Tying my hands up? Isn't that a little crude, Liv?

OLIVIA

Be quiet.

SAM

Is it me, or does Bobby seem a little confused?

OLIVIA

I said be quiet.

SAM   Oh I see . . . He doesn't know. You haven't
               told him about it have you? I thought
               husband and wife were meant to tell each
               other everything? Keeping it to yourself,
               huh? An escape clause in case you wake
               up five years down the line and realise you
               don't want him anymore.

OLIVIA   Shut up!

SAM   Oh, Olivia. Keeping secrets from your
               husband. This marriage hasn't got off on the
               right foot, has it?

OLIVIA   He doesn't need to know.

SAM   I think he does. His quiet little life has been
               interrupted. He's witnessed a murder, he's
               disturbed material evidence and now he has
               a man tied up and threatened at gunpoint
               by his wife. I think he has a right to know,
               don't you?

               (ROBERT *opens the French windows and
               enters, holding some rope.*)

ROBERT   This is all I could find.

               (ROBERT *closes the doors after himself.*)

OLIVIA   Tie him up, Robert. Hands behind his back.
               Tie them tightly.

               (*He ties up* SAM's *hands behind his back.*)

SAM   Quite the pair of master criminals, aren't
               we?

ROBERT   What the hell is going on?

SAM   I think you should tell him, Liv. Maybe start
            with the fact I saved both your lives.

ROBERT   I find that hard to believe.

SAM   Hard or not, it's the truth. The guy I
            strangled and is now at the bottom of the
            cliff, is a criminal. Intent on coming here,
            stealing something very precious and killing
            you both. That's the truth. Isn't it, Liv?

OLIVIA   That's what you'd have us believe.

SAM   Oh, come on, you know it's true. Whether
            you trust me or not, you know he came here
            to steal the diamond. He stole the necklace
            from me, for God's sake!

ROBERT   Necklace? What necklace?

SAM   Will you, or will I?

            (OLIVIA still keeping the gun pointing at
            SAM.)

            Looks like it's been left up to me. How's
            your Napoleonic history, Bobby? Well,
            let me enlighten you. In 1810, Napoleon
            Bonaparte married Marie Louise of Austria,
            a double grandniece of Marie Antoinette.
            Keen to impress his new in-laws, he
            produced a necklace, designed and made
            especially for Marie Louise. It was stunning.
            Three stones; a ruby on the right, a sapphire
            on the left and in the middle a beautiful,
            large, diamond. Red, white and blue. The
            Tricolour necklace.

            Now this is the important bit. For security
            reasons the stones could slip in and out of

the clasps that held them. Only the stones
that were designed for that necklace would
ever fit that necklace.

Marie Louise kept it her whole life. When
Napoleon went into exile on Elba, she
returned to the city of her birth, Vienna.
The necklace stayed there, in the vaults of
the Hofburg Palace until 1945 when the
Soviets besieged the then German occupied
city.

No one quite knows where it went then;
stolen, probably by a fleeing German
soldier. It disappeared until 1998 when it
turned up at auction and was bought by the
Napoleonic fanatic Charles Harper-Radley,
Ninth Earl of Warwick. From then on, it
stayed in Harper-Radley's collection, at
Radley Hall, here in England. Until just over
a year ago.

ROBERT   What happened a year ago?

SAM   I stole it.

ROBERT   You surprise me.

SAM   I worked my way into Radley Hall, past the
              security and stole it.

ROBERT   But how does this involve Olivia? She didn't
              steal anything.

SAM   Oh, but she did. The diamond.

ROBERT   What?

SAM   When I told Olivia what happened, she lost
              the plot. You see, all went well, except . . .

for the small matter of me having to kill
someone. The Ninth Earl of Warwick, as it
happened.

ROBERT   It was you? I remember it on the news. You
murdered him?

SAM   Suspicious death. That's what the coroner
said. Police never found anything to trace.
But yes, it was me. I didn't know he'd be
there. I thought he was in London. But
there he was . . . coughing and spluttering
into his oxygen mask. The bloke may have
been dying, but he'd still seen me, could
still identify me. So I put my hand over
his mouth and he was dead in less than a
minute.

ROBERT   Oh my God.

SAM   I decided to place the necklace in a secure
vault in Switzerland, I split the stones to
minimise risk and gave her the diamond to
look after. We were meant to meet in Zurich
a few days later. Guess what? She never
turned up. That's love and trust for you.

ROBERT   So, when we met, you were on the run from
him, with the diamond?

(OLIVIA *nods*.)

But why didn't you tell me? Why didn't you
say something?

SAM   Because she's greedy. She wants that
diamond all to herself.

OLIVIA   That's not true!

ROBERT	And you've still got it? Somewhere in this house?
OLIVIA	Yes.
ROBERT	Where, for God's sake?
OLIVIA	I can't tell you, not until we've dealt with Sam.
ROBERT	We have to call the police.
SAM	Don't be so stupid. All they'll find are two hysterical people with a dead man at the bottom of their garden, a man tied up in a chair and a stolen diamond in their possession.
ROBERT	We could explain.
SAM	Really? Because that's all the police will see. You moved the body, not me.
OLIVIA	It's true, Robert.
ROBERT	And this bloke Ramsay . . .?
SAM	A crook, like me. I didn't steal the necklace to wear; I stole it to sell it. So it'll be better for all of us if Liv tells me where the diamond is and I'll leave your lives forever.
OLIVIA	Or we get rid of you, forever.
	(*She raises the gun.*)
ROBERT	No!
SAM	Oh come off it! She's not going to kill me.

OLIVIA   Why not?

SAM   It's not in your blood, Liv, you wouldn't do
              it. You don't have the nerves.

OLIVIA   No, Sam, You're making the same mistake
              as before. You've underestimated me.

SAM   You couldn't kill me. You still love me.
              Wouldn't you rather live the life of luxury
              with me? It would be a lot more fun.

OLIVIA   No, Sam, it wouldn't.

SAM   You won't kill me. You can't kill. To do
              that, you'd have to be a criminal just like
              me. And you've got a lot to learn before that
              happens.

OLIVIA   Oh really?

              (*She walks right up to him with the gun
              towards his head.*)

SAM   Yes. And I'd say that the first thing you
              need to learn; is always check that you're
              victim's hands are properly tied.

              (SAM *pulls his hands from behind his back
              and quickly wrestles the gun from her
              hands. He throws her onto the chair,* ROBERT
              goes to attack him.)

SAM   (*pointing the gun at him*) No, Bobby, no!
              I don't need you. I don't need you at all. I
              can easily put a bullet between those puppy
              dog eyes of yours and it would make no
              difference. So sit down and shut the hell
              up! Right, enough of these stupid games.
              Where's the diamond, Olivia? Tell me

and I'll go. Leave you alone forever. So,
be a good girl and tell me . . . where's the
diamond?

OLIVIA   (*coolly*) It's no use, Sam. You don't scare me
              anymore. I'm immune to your charm and
              immune to your threats. Kill me? What good
              would that do? You wouldn't be any closer
              to finding where I've put it. Anyhow, I mean
              too much to you. Even if you hate me right
              now, that's only because you loved me once.

              (*Pause.* SAM *lowers the gun.*)

SAM   You know, you're right. I don't think I
              could kill you. Not my schnuffle face.
              Maybe you've beaten me. Maybe I've
              underestimated you. I do still love you and
              that's the greatest weapon you have.

              (*Pause.*)

              But, the question I have to ask is . . . how
              much do you love that diamond?

OLIVIA   I don't understand.

SAM   It's been over a year now, it's long enough
              for you to have become . . . obsessed by it.
              Entranced by it. Even when you found out
              what I'd done, I saw in your eyes, you were
              swept away with love for that diamond.

              (SAM *moves over towards* ROBERT. OLIVIA
              doesn't reply.)

SAM   But how much do you love it compared to,
              let's say . . .

              (SAM *slowly puts the gun to* ROBERT's *head.*)

Robert . . . How much do you love it, then?
Where's the diamond, Olivia?

ROBERT   Oh, God. Please, no.

OLIVIA   Sam . . . no, he has nothing to do with this.

SAM   Nothing to do with it? He's your husband.
He has a hell of a lot to do with it.
Especially if he's about to die.

OLIVIA   Please, Sam, I beg you . . . let Robert go.

SAM   Where is it, Olivia?

ROBERT   Just tell him, tell him now.

OLIVIA   You won't kill Robert, I know you won't!

SAM   Trust me, I will and I'll have no qualms in
doing so . . . where is the bloody diamond?

ROBERT   For God's sake, Olivia, he's got a gun to my
head.

SAM   Listen to your darling husband, he's talking
sense.

OLIVIA   Don't you understand? I can't tell him, we
can't let him win!

SAM   Winning, losing . . . what does it matter? All
I want is the diamond, tell me and no one
has to die.

OLIVIA   Two people have already died, Sam! Don't
kill again, it's not worth it.

SAM   It bloody well is!

ROBERT	Just tell him!
OLIVIA	No, Robert, he won't kill you, I know he won't.
SAM	Bobby, have you ever wondered what death is like?
ROBERT	Oh God . . .
SAM	Personally, I don't believe in a life after death. How about you? Well, you're about to find out.
ROBERT	(*a final, almost pathetic plea*) Olivia . . .
SAM	You're leaving me with no choice, Liv . . . where is it?
OLIVIA	Sam! No!
SAM	Sorry Bobby . . . it's been a pleasure.
	(SAM *turns to* ROBERT *with the gun raised, pulls the trigger and the gun goes off.* ROBERT *falls onto the sofa, face down.*)
OLIVIA	Oh God, no . . . Please no . . .
	(*She runs towards the body, but* SAM *grabs her and pushes her onto the floor.*)
SAM	This is no time for grieving . . . you've made the mistake this time, Liv. You underestimated me.
	(OLIVIA *crawls over to* ROBERT *and tugs at his leg.*)
OLIVIA	You bastard! Robert, Robert . . . please . . .

(*As she sobs,* ROBERT, *lying dead on the sofa starts . . .*)

ROBERT   (*Laughing.*)

(OLIVIA *gradually stops crying and looks up.* ROBERT *jumps up . . .*)

ROBERT   Boo!

(OLIVIA *still on the floor recoils away from* ROBERT *staring at him in disbelief and shock as* ROBERT *rises up, laughing. Both* ROBERT *and* SAM *laugh heartily and hug.*)

SAM   As I guessed; she loves the diamond more than she loves you. Oh, Liv, meet Bobby . . . my little brother. And your ex-husband.

(*They laugh again.*)

For a minute, I thought you were really going to tie my hands, you little sod!

ROBERT   Of course I wouldn't. It's me.

(SAM *takes the bullets from the gun.*)

SAM   At least now we can have a real threat. I felt like a right fraud with blanks.

(*He reaches into an inside pocket and pulls out some more bullets and puts them in the gun (Duds).*)

ROBERT   What a bitch! I didn't think we'd have to go this far.

SAM   I should've put some money on it. You'd
               know that she'd push us all the way. Well
               done, Liv!

OLIVIA   What . . . what's . . . ?

SAM   Oh, I'm sorry, let me explain. Bobby and
               me, we're not just brothers, we're best
               friends. We share . . . absolutely everything.
               We've always been there for each other.

OLIVIA   I don't understand. You're Robert Chappell.

ROBERT   Afraid not. Robert Stone actually.

OLIVIA   Brothers? But . . . you mean . . .
               (*Realisation.*) Bobby . . .

SAM   Bobby . . . exactly. Ring a few bells? When
               we were together enjoying our blissful
               romance, remember I mentioned a little
               brother? Staying at her Majesty's pleasure in
               a fabulous little hostel near Exeter?

OLIVIA   My God . . .

ROBERT   You know, I think she's got it.

SAM   Bobby here, changing the habit of a
               lifetime, behaved himself impeccably and
               was released from prison just in time to
               help out his big brother. You see, I was at a
               loss, but he had just the plan. And for a cut
               of the money he came up with this whole
               enterprise.

ROBERT   So I followed you. We'd never met and he
               knew I could, let's say, be your type. The
               kind of guy you'd fall for. And you did fall
               for it, hook, line and sinker.

SAM   I was never worried . . . you were married
                   to him. The diamond was safe. In the
                   possession of my brother and my sister-in-
                   law! You might as well have been married to
                   me.

OLIVIA   I don't . . . but . . . my God . . .

ROBERT   Thing is, Liv, you can't imagine how bored
                   I've been. A hotel, here? Telling you I
                   loved you. It's been a nightmare, everyday
                   pretending. Every day . . . looking for the
                   bloody diamond. Sam can't believe I haven't
                   found it yet, but I haven't. We need the
                   diamond, Liv, otherwise Victor's going to be
                   very disappointed.

SAM   And Victor's not the kind of guy you want to
                   disappoint.

OLIVIA   Well, that's your problem for getting
                   involved with a guy like Victor.

ROBERT   No, it's your problem for having the
                   diamond!

SAM   Calm down, Bobby. She's going to tell us.
                   She's got no choice.

OLIVIA   I have. I can die. You're going to have to kill
                   me anyway. Go ahead! I've got nothing to
                   live for.

SAM   I'm disappointed, Liv.

                   (*Beat.*)

                   Bobby . . . the necklace?

ROBERT   What?

SAM   The necklace! Where is it?

ROBERT   I saw him put in in his jacket . . .

SAM   Go on then.

               (ROBERT *goes to* RAMSAY's *jacket that is
               hanging in the hallway, rifles through the
               pocket and finds the jewellery case.*)

ROBERT   Here.

               (*He throws the box to him.* SAM *opens it.*)

SAM   Is this some kind of joke?

ROBERT   What do you mean?

SAM   It's not here.

ROBERT   What?

SAM   Where is it?

ROBERT   I . . . don't know.

               (SAM *points the gun at* OLIVIA.)

SAM   Liv?

OLIVIA   I haven't touched it.

ROBERT   She hasn't, I've been with her all night.

SAM   You left the house twice. Once to check
               outside and then to get firewood.

ROBERT   Yeah I know, but . . .

SAM   But nothing. Your little wife here could
              easily have taken it. Liv, come on, you've
              admitted defeat, where is the necklace?

OLIVIA   I haven't touched it. I want nothing to do
              with it.

              (SAM *calms down and goes over to* OLIVIA,
              very cool.)

SAM   Listen, if you want nothing to do with it,
              the best thing you can do is hand it and the
              diamond over.

              (*She goes to protest.*)

              If we don't deliver the necklace to Victor in
              Paris by tomorrow night, unspeakable things
              are going to happen to us. He will find us,
              trust me. He knows we're here.

OLIVIA   He knows?

SAM   Of course.

OLIVIA   In our hotel?

SAM   Yes, he wanted to know everything. And
              he'll come for you too. I've no problem
              telling him you're the reason his necklace
              hasn't been delivered. Understand? Time is
              running out, Liv and so is my patience.

OLIVIA   I haven't touched the necklace Sam. I
              promise.

              (*Pause.*)

SAM   I believe her. He's still got it. I told you to
              keep an eye on him!

ROBERT   I didn't know he'd nicked it off you did I?
                  As far as I knew everything was going to
                  plan!

SAM   Right, well it's not as if he can put up a
                  fight. Go and get it back. Go through his
                  pockets, it'll be there.

ROBERT   It's freezing out there.

SAM   (*pointedly*) I know . . . I walked here.

                  (ROBERT *goes to the French windows, opens
                  the doors and then turns back . . .*)

ROBERT   Liv, I love you.

                  (*He mockingly blows her a kiss.*)

SAM   Get out!

                  (ROBERT *exits, laughing and closing the
                  doors after himself.* SAM *pours himself a
                  whisky.*)

SAM   Fancy a drink?

                  (*She shakes her head.* SAM *downs the drink
                  in one and grimaces. He inspects the bottle.*)

OLIVIA   Go to hell.

SAM   I may, but at least I'll be rich.

OLIVIA   Is that all that matters to you?

SAM   No. Something else matters to me.

OLIVIA   And what's that?

SAM   To hurt you, like you hurt me. You made a
           fool of me, Liv. You betrayed what we had.
           Bobby was amazing, don't you think? You
           must've hidden it somewhere pretty damn
           good. But I need that diamond, Liv.

           (*She simply stares into space.*)

OLIVIA   If I give it to you, will you leave me alone?
           Forever? You can have your blood money,
           but leave me alone. I don't want to know
           where you're going. I don't want to tell the
           police. I just want to be alone. Quietly. I'm
           tired, Sam.

SAM   Of course. If that's what you want . . . I'll
           leave you alone.

OLIVIA   Do you promise?

SAM   I don't want to kill you, Liv.

OLIVIA   You promise?

SAM   I promise.

           (*She stops, and suddenly starts to laugh.*)

OLIVIA   (*laughing*) I must be mad. Why should I
           trust you? You'll kill me anyway. I'll tell
           you where the diamond is and you'll kill me.

SAM   I won't, I promised.

           (OLIVIA *stares at him in silence. She goes
           towards the drinks cabinet. Suddenly*
           RAMSAY *appears behind at the French
           windows.*)

OLIVIA   (*Scream!*)

(*He throws the doors open and attacks* SAM. *They struggle for a few moments before* SAM *is overpowered.* RAMSAY *forces him to the floor, and with the poker he suffocates* SAM . . . RAMSAY *turns to* OLIVIA.)

OLIVIA   Ramsay? But . . . but . . . you're . . .

RAMSAY   I hate to disappoint. I must admit, everything went dark for a while. Woke up about half an hour later covered in rope at the bottom of the cliff face. Trying to make it look like an accident. Bit amateur. If you really want to fake a climbing accident, you have to break the neck.

(RAMSAY *takes* SAM'S *head and in one quick movement and with a stomach-churning crack, he breaks his neck. He starts moving the body . . .*)

Come on, give me a hand.

(OLIVIA *doesn't move.*)

RAMSAY   Olivia!

(OLIVIA, *slightly confused, doesn't know what to do.*)

Take his legs.

(OLIVIA *moves over and takes* SAM'S *legs, helps* RAMSAY *drag the body to the French windows. He then moves the body just outside the doors, out of sight.*)

RAMSAY   I'll put him at the bottom of the cliff later.

(RAMSAY *re-enters and closes French windows and the curtains.*)

OLIVIA   Where's Robert?

RAMSAY   I was outside waiting for my chance when he came out. I ran up to him to see if he was all right and to ask after you. You should have seen the look in his eyes . . . and then out of nowhere he attacked me.

OLIVIA   What did you do?

RAMSAY   The same as I did to Sam, I'm afraid.

OLIVIA   Oh my God.

RAMSAY   I didn't know . . .

OLIVIA   He was Sam's brother.

RAMSAY   Brother? You're joking.

OLIVIA   They'd set it all up.

RAMSAY   To get the diamond. My God, so your whole marriage . . .

OLIVIA   Was a lie.

RAMSAY   I'm sorry. Clever.

OLIVIA   You're as bad as them. You're only here for the diamond as well.

RAMSAY   True . . . but at least I have the claim that it's rightfully mine.

OLIVIA   How?

RAMSAY	(*putting out his hand*) Ramsay Harper-Radley. Tenth Earl of Warwick. A pleasure to meet you.
OLIVIA	What?
RAMSAY	My father was murdered for his most treasured possession, the Tricolour Necklace, by the man who's now lying outside.
OLIVIA	Why should I believe you?
RAMSAY	I've been searching for the necklace for over a year. By the time of my father's death I was living in New Zealand, fulfilling a stupid dream. Even though he was ill, he insisted that I still go. He was a wonderful man, full of life and adventure and he wanted me to be the same. I wanted to come home and tell him all about it, to cheer him up. I never got that chance; he was murdered three weeks before I was due to come back. Since then, I've watched the inept police come up with nothing so I vowed to return the necklace to its proper home, my home. Radley Hall. It's all I can do for my father now.

(*She looks unsure.* RAMSAY *produces a photo from his wallet.*)

RAMSAY	That's my father. Standing on the lawn infront of Radley Hall. I took it just before I left for New Zealand.

(*Pause.*)

OLIVIA	It's really yours? The necklace?

RAMSAY   My family's, yes.

OLIVIA   We should phone the police?

RAMSAY   And say what? I murdered two men, and
            hope an aristocratic title will get me off?
            No, I don't want to involve the police at all.
            They've lost interest in the case. Olivia, I
            didn't want to kill anyone, but it was them
            or me.

OLIVIA   But what about Sam and Robert?

RAMSAY   I'll do the dirty work. They both have
            broken necks and they'll both look as if they
            died climbing. All you have to do is report
            your husband missing. That he hasn't come
            back from his winter climb with his brother.
            In this wind, it's easy to be blown off the
            cliff face . . . and when you're attached to
            someone else on a rope . . .? Well, it's an
            accident waiting to happen.

OLIVIA   What about their buyer? This Victor?

RAMSAY   Yes, I know about Victor. It's through him I
            found out about Sam.

OLIVIA   How?

RAMSAY   Because I'm Victor.

OLIVIA   What?

RAMSAY   I invented a rich, underworld collector to
            lure Sam. I realised there was no point
            trying to be some sort of have-a-go amateur
            sleuth. They only exist in fiction. So I
            changed my spots. The necklace was lost in
            the underworld, so I joined the underworld.

	Victor was born. Sam was so desperate to sell the thing that all it took was a few enquiries and a visit posing as a go-between, to make him lead me all the way to the missing diamond.

OLIVIA   And then you tried to kill him on the mountainside?

RAMSAY   Is that what he told you? All I did was knock him out. I thought a night up in the mountains would teach him a lesson.

OLIVIA   Or freeze him to death.

RAMSAY   He was my father's murderer so I wasn't that sympathetic.

OLIVIA   No, I suppose not.

RAMSAY   I also thought, that I'd find the diamond quite quickly once I got here. But you're too smart for that.

(Pause.)

OLIVIA   I need a drink.

(OLIVIA *moves over to the bar.*)

Whisky?

RAMSAY   Please.

(OLIVIA *pours a whisky for him and one for herself in her usual glass. Both glasses are on top of the cabinet. They both take a sip in silence,* OLIVIA *closes her eyes and relishes it,* RAMSAY *keeps his eyes on her.*)

OLIVIA   Tonight, well . . . it's all been . . .

RAMSAY   I can imagine.

OLIVIA   To tell you the truth, I'll be glad to see the
            back of the diamond. I've never really been
            able to relax. I've always been waiting. And
            now Sam's dead and the terrible thing is,
            seeing his body there, it didn't disgust me.

RAMSAY   No, that's a true sign of hate.

OLIVIA   I suppose it is.

RAMSAY   And Robert?

OLIVIA   Robert? I don't know how I feel about that
            yet.

RAMSAY   It'll take time.

OLIVIA   Yes.

RAMSAY   Feel free to come to Radley Hall. Whenever
            you want. For as long as you want.

OLIVIA   Thank you. I don't think I can stay here.

            (*Pause.*)

RAMSAY   I meant what I said earlier, you know.

OLIVIA   What?

RAMSAY   I do think you're very beautiful.

OLIVIA   Is now the time to be paying compliments?

RAMSAY   I think this is the perfect time.

(*They smile and hold each other's gaze for a moment.* OLIVIA *looks at her glass then breaks away from* RAMSAY.)

OLIVIA   My father was a terrible gambler.

RAMSAY   I'm sorry?

OLIVIA   He would bet on anything. He used to sell our possessions to fund it. Ornaments, furniture, anything. Eventually, he moved onto my mother's jewellery. She knew, but she couldn't stop him. But her favourite piece was a diamond broach she bought in Rome before they met. She couldn't bear to see him sell that. To hide it from him, she had something made that would disguise the broach perfectly. Somewhere he'd never think of looking. The funny thing was, it was under his nose all the time.

(OLIVIA *finishes her drink in one then takes the glass, turns it over and unscrews the base. It comes off. She puts out her hand and tips the base and a good sized diamond falls out into her hand. She offers it to* RAMSAY. *He takes it and holds it up . . .*)

RAMSAY   My God, I've got it. After all this time, I've got it.

(RAMSAY *fishes out the necklace out of his pocket. He gently slips the stone back into the clasp of necklace.*)

Look, just look how beautiful it is.

OLIVIA   It's been over a year since it was complete. The way it should be.

RAMSAY   The way it should be, yes. Thank you.

OLIVIA   No need. It's come back to its proper home.

RAMSAY   Yes.

             (*Pause.*)

RAMSAY   Put it on.

OLIVIA   What?

RAMSAY   I told you . . . you're beautiful. You'd
             complement each other.

             (*He approaches her, stands behind her and
             puts the necklace around her neck.*)

RAMSAY   Amazing to think this was once around the
             neck of Marie Louise.

OLIVIA   Sam would never let me wear it.

RAMSAY   I'm not Sam.

OLIVIA   No, no you're not.

             (*Another moment together . . .*)

             It's true.

             (OLIVIA *turns and moves over to the mirror.*)

RAMSAY   What?

OLIVIA   Sam was right. After holding onto this
             diamond for so long, I do love it, covet it
             even. And now, wearing the whole necklace
             as one, well . . . do I sound silly?

RAMSAY	Not at all.
OLIVIA	It's going to be hard to say goodbye to.
RAMSAY	(*with a wry smile*) Radley Hall is open to the public, visit anytime you like.
OLIVIA	Thank you.
RAMSAY	Yes. Well, the visitors help. You won't believe how much it costs to run a place the size of Radley. But I'd prefer it . . .
OLIVIA	What?
RAMSAY	. . . if you didn't come as a visitor.
	(*Pause. After a moment* OLIVIA *turns away from him.*)
RAMSAY	Sorry, I didn't mean to . . .
OLIVIA	No, no it's fine. It's just that it's all . . . been, I . . .
RAMSAY	I know, I know.
	(OLIVIA *fiddles with the necklace and looks at herself again in the mirror. She pauses, sees the gun on the table, she picks it up.*)
RAMSAY	What are you doing? Olivia?
	(*Pause. Threat.*)
OLIVIA	I'm not sure I like having a loaded gun in the house.
RAMSAY	(*relieved*) No, me neither. Here.

(She hands him the gun, he empties the bullets and puts them in his pocket.)

RAMSAY   I'll put the whole lot into the lake.

OLIVIA   Thank you.

RAMSAY   Now, you need some rest . . . Why don't you go to bed. I'll stay here until morning. I'll move Sam's body and get rid of the gun.

OLIVIA   You won't leave me?

RAMSAY   I'll be back before you know it. I'll even cook breakfast. *(Indicating the necklace.)* You'd better give me that back.

(RAMSAY helps her with the necklace. She takes the necklace off and hands it to him.)

OLIVIA   I wouldn't want to sleep in it anyway.

(She turns and exits through to the bedrooms. RAMSAY gives her a moment to go. He takes out the bullets from his pocket and puts them in the gun just as . . .)

OLIVIA   *(entering)* I thought I might take a drink . . .

(She stops on seeing RAMSAY loading the gun.)

OLIVIA   . . . Upstairs.

(Pause.)

RAMSAY   Sure.

(He smiles, puts the gun back down on the table, not sure if she's seen anything and

walks over, in silence, to pour a drink. With his back to her . . .)

OLIVIA   I nearly died tonight.

RAMSAY   I know.

OLIVIA   Sam would have killed me. I was too much of a threat, wasn't I?

RAMSAY   I'm afraid so. Yes. But don't trouble yourself, take this . . . (*Indicating the drink.*) . . . and get some rest.

              (*Pause. She goes to take the drink but stops . . .)*

OLIVIA   Radley Hall is open to the public . . .

RAMSAY   That's right.

OLIVIA   Your photo. The one of your father . . .

RAMSAY   Uh huh?

OLIVIA   The coat of arms above the front door of the house, is that the family crest?

RAMSAY   Yes.

OLIVIA   It's very beautiful. But I couldn't make out the writing. What does it say?

RAMSAY   Oh . . . Something or other in Latin.

OLIVIA   But Ramsay?

RAMSAY   Yes?

OLIVIA   There isn't a coat of arms above the door.

(*Pause. They both dash for the gun, there
is a struggle, the gun can't be seen between
their bodies. They fall to the floor,* RAMSAY
on top of her. The gun goes off. OLIVIA
pushes and rolls RAMSAY *off her body. He's
dead. Silence.* OLIVIA *stands over the body.*)

OLIVIA   (*to herself*) I didn't kill him. It was his
              finger on the trigger, not mine. He was
              trying to kill me. There are three dead
              people and I didn't kill one of them.

              (OLIVIA *moves over to get the necklace.
              She slowly puts it on and moves over to the
              mirror admiring herself. The phone rings.
              With some trepidation she answers it* . . .)

OLIVIA   Hello? Who is this? Victor? Of course . . .
              (*She looks at the body on the floor.*) Sneaky
              bastard. Oh, nothing. Ramsay? Yes, but he
              can't come to the phone right now. Well,
              I'm afraid your 'go-between' planned on
              keeping the necklace all to himself. You
              won't have to do that Victor . . . he's already
              dead. It doesn't matter who I am, all that
              matters is the necklace. Yes, it's safe. Of
              course, it's still for sale. How much? Yes,
              yes that sounds . . . fine. I can be in Paris
              by tomorrow afternoon. Tell me when and
              where.

              (OLIVIA *jots down the info.*)

              Yes, I've got that. I'll expect all money
              on delivery. Good. I look forward to it.
              But Victor, don't make the same mistake
              as everybody else. It's very easy to
              underestimate a woman.

              (*She puts the phone down and goes over to
              her glass. She screws it back together and*

*pours herself a drink. She then puts some
music on; "Somethin' Stupid" plays once
again and she smiles, takes a sip of her
drink and slowly dances to CS. Music swells
and slow fade to blackout.)*